R. A. JONICKI

15 Year Retirement Plan Using Real Estate

A low cost, low stress way to retire quickly with Real Estate.

This book was professionally typeset on Reedsy.
Find out more at reedsy.com

Contents

INTRODUCTION

Hi All! I am excited to talk to you today about this concept of retiring in 15 years with a six-figure, non-taxable yearly income! Most people have to work 30 to 50 years and then pray that their 401k or other retirement plan has enough money to sustain them through the rest of their life. How would you like to have something that is guaranteed to sustain you, replenishing itself every year, instead of dwindling down as time goes by? And instead of paying tens of thousands of dollars to the people out there promising to teach you real estate investing, something that you may not even enjoy or have been called to do for your path in life, you can do and work in whatever industry or line of work that you chose for yourself and still retire in 15 years?

I have been a United States real estate investor since 2004. I made it through the housing bubble in 2008-2009. I grew to over 220 units in 12 years time. I sat on the Board of the local Real Estate Investors Association and I was a coach in the local real estate mastermind group. I did enjoy this part of my life.

But, I became tired of tenant excuses for late rent, evicting people close to holidays and the ever present clogged toilets and sinks. I ultimately realized I didn't have to grow that big to have a retirement. I just didn't know what else to do because I had invested those tens of thousands ($88,000.00 to be exact when I checked into it once) to learn real estate investing and so I just kept going.

You, my dear friend, can do the job you want to do, or what you feel you were called to do, and I can show you how to have the greatest wealth making machine in history help you retire in just 15 years. Were you aware that 90% of millionaires either made their money in real estate or hold their money in real estate? That tells you a lot about the tax benefits of real estate. But enough of talking about taxes! I don't want your eyes to glaze over and you put this book down. You see, I KNOW if you put the plan outlined in this book into action, you will be living your life on your terms in as short as 15 years from now.

I also want to be clear that this plan is laid out for the United States. I do not know how the real estate market works in other countries or, when I talk about taxes, again, I do not know what the rules are in other countries.

Let's get started!

THE FOUNDATION

This book assumes you are already working the job of your choice. Hopefully it's one you enjoy and like to do as we do expect you to continue to work it for the next 15 years.

This book also assumes you have the credit score to be able to handle buying a house, or you are willing to do what you need to do to get your score where it needs to be. Maybe you already own a house, the one you live in. If you don't, that is the first thing you must do. Stop throwing away money on rent when you can be paying down your own mortgage.

First thing you need to do is find and work with a mortgage broker. They can shop several different mortgage companies to find one that is best for you and your situation. A broker can pull your credit one time to shop several different mortgage companies with it. They can also tell you what you need to do to help quickly increase your score, if needed. They will be your best friend through the next 15 years. Talk to one today. It may take a few months to get your score where you need it or have the down payment that you will need. Get the facts straight from the broker so you know what you need to work towards, if anything. Too many people assume they need so much more than they have that they don't even find out for sure.

If you have a small town bank that likes to do mortgages in their community, you can go that route also. I'm not a fan of the bigger banks because they may give you one loan for your own home but then they may want to cut you off if you try for another home loan or two. They are larger and can cherry pick who they give loans to, so you'll have to have a strong credit standing to use them. Too many hits on your credit can pull down your score if one place says no then you go to another and another. This is why I choose to use a mortgage broker. You can even tell them your plan and they can help give you tips of what to do and not do to keep you ready as you grow your retirement.

So year one, buy yourself a house. If you don't own one for yourself, this will be your home. Know that your 15 years to retirement may actually be 16 as you add this foundation block. If you do own one for yourself, good for you! You are on the right track in life, now let's expand on that.

It's up to you if you choose a fixer upper or a move-in ready one. Remember, you have a job and I want to make this as hands off and as painless as possible, but if you buy one with equity, that is always nice and usually foreclosures needing a little TLC will get you instant equity.

If a fixer upper, DO NOT DO major repairs. You will be getting in over your head. My job is not to teach you the training of being a fix and flip real estate investor. If you want to take on doing some fresh paint or replace a bathroom vanity or two, fine. There are lots of contractors and handymen out there to make extremely short work of this for you. Just make sure you don't pay them until after the job is complete. This is my one and only warning to you in dealing with handymen. If someone needs money upfront for materials or anything else, move on. Please, please, please listen to me on this. Do not use a friend who can do it.

Don't try to do it yourself. Painting sounds easy until you actually do it. Can you believe I actually bought a house where the walls weren't painted all the way to the ceiling? After trying unsuccessfully to paint the edging between the ceiling and the wall in one room, they gave up and literally had scalloped edging painted with a roller close to the ceiling and then they stopped. They lived in their house this way until I took it off their hands because they couldn't find a buyer with a Realtor. You can bet I received some equity with this deal all because they tried to do something their self and were unsuccessful.

If you buy a move-in ready house, make sure you don't overpay. Let your Realtor know you are buying a rental property. You want a good deal that makes sense, not an overpriced house with nice finishes that you love. You won't be living there. And trust me, after a couple of years with tenants, those finishes won't look like the ones you fell in love with. Bring a level-headed friend or spouse with you when you go to look at each potential house. And promise each other to help keep the other from falling in love with the house. And have the Realtor help you. Let them know you want a RENT READY house. You will not pay for upgraded finishes so they shouldn't even show you those places. You can only charge rent for what the neighborhood supports. Trying to get more will only cause you to have a higher tenant turn rate. There are costs involved each time a tenant moves out. There will always be a tenant turn rate, but don't encourage a higher one by not listening to me. Check your emotional button at the door when you walk into a potential house with your Realtor.

THE DUE DILIGENCE

Zillow.com does pretty good at giving rent estimates if you type in the property address, especially in bigger towns and cities. Check local Craigslist.org listings for rentals currently on the market and what they are asking. Rentometer.com can also help you when selecting what you should charge for rent. If you've selected a property manager that you are going to use, you can have them give you a quote on what they would charge for rent. Do this during your due diligence period when selecting a house. Do not close on a house then try to figure out what you can rent it for. You may have just paid more for a house then you can get out of it.

Do not trust Zillow for verifying a sale price. The company may improve over time, but I didn't use it for guesstimating best sale prices and I wouldn't recommend that you do so either. Use your Realtor instead to help you choose the perfect offer. They should only be showing you only good rental deals if you were precise in telling them what you are looking for. They will also be able to tell you if the market can support an offer below sale price or not.

I would not buy in bad neighborhoods, the ones that are always on the news. The houses may be cheaper in those neighborhoods but the headaches are not.

Find the median price point for your town or city. Your Realtor can help you with that. Then look for ones that are good deals, like the lower to mid point of the median price point. As a real estate investor, we were always taught the 1% rule. Your rent price should be approximately 1% of the purchase price. Example, a hundred thousand dollar house should rent for one thousand dollars. I won't lie, this is not easy to do. I was happy making .09% most of the time. This is still hard to do if you are not a real estate investor, spending thousands of dollars each month in marketing to bring you the best of the best deals. But it is something that you can aim for. Obviously you do not want to buy a $500,000 house that you can only rent for $1,800. Select a different house.

Okay, if this is your first house, your house, the mortgage broker would have told you the price point that you qualify for and the Realtor would have shown you ones that would work for you. Hopefully you selected one on the lower end of your price range so you won't be cash poor because you bought too much house. Remember, you will need to be able to put aside savings so you have down payment on your next house in a year. In fifteen years you can be extravagant, sacrifice now so you can have the life you want in 15 years while everyone else is still living paycheck to paycheck to pay for everything they wanted "now."

If this is your home, you can take a 30 year mortgage out. That will keep your payments low and will allow you to save for your next down payment. Know that your fifteen years to retirement won't begin until next year. If it's your second house, we want you to close with a 15 year, fixed rate mortgage.

When you sign on the dotted line and the house becomes yours, we call this the closing.

AFTER THE CLOSING

We were taught as real estate investors to get your payments as low as possible and aim for a $250 a month cash flow per property. Guess what? $250 a month is only $3,000 a year. How many properties would you need to own to be able to live comfortably on this real estate investing thing? And if a furnace goes out or you need a new roof for a particular property, that $3,000 is gone for that year and probably some of the next year's income to boot. Heck, what if the tenant moves out and their dog totally wrecks the carpets and you need to replace the flooring? Do you see where I'm going with this? I say don't worry about the cash flow. Let the tenant pay for the mortgage and most of the small repairs with the rent they pay. If you have to help with an expense here and there through the years, so be it. You are working the job you love, remember? And you are willing to sacrifice now for the life you will have in 15 years and every year past that while most people are still trying to get there.

If this is your second house, your rental house, it's time to get it on the market to find that tenant. The way I envision this for you is to have a property manager. Make sure you shop around as there are different levels of property management and different pricing. And remember, as with everything in life, you usually get what you pay for. Ask their vacancy rate when you are considering them. And how long it takes them on average to do a tenant turn. Run from anyone who cannot get a tenant turn handled in less than 2 weeks. The longer your property sits vacant, the more money you lose.

Some people may want to save that property management fee by managing it themselves. I really don't have a problem with this except for two things, putting in the tenant and getting the tenant out. Some property managers will find you a qualified tenant, and let you handle tenant calls for repairs, etc as well as collecting the rent. Make sure they will also file an eviction for you if things go south with your tenant.

The reason I say to have a professional rental company find you a qualified tenant is because of the word "qualified." Nothing is more heart-breaking than putting a new tenant into your property only to never receive another penny from them. They lied about their job. They lied about their credit. They lied about how many people would be living there. They lied about their drug charges. They lied. An experienced property management company has dealt with this time and time again. They know all the supporting documents to collect. They have the credentials to do a criminal background check and credit check. Use them or stop reading this book because you will probably not successfully get to the 15th year.

That also becomes true for evictions. Most property managers start eviction proceedings on schedule with the laws in your State. Tell them immediately when you do not collect the rent if you are managing everything else yourself. The tenant will tell you they will pay you "Friday on payday," three days after the eviction proceedings should have started. You wait because it's a hassle filling out the eviction paperwork. On Friday evening, they'll text you that they didn't make it to the bank to cash their check because they worked late. Who has to deposit their check any more these days?! But it's the weekend anyway so you wait. Now it's Tuesday morning a week later and you are just now starting the eviction process. You lost another week's rent and you still have to do the eviction anyway. And guess what, if you started the process exactly when you should have, and they do come up with the rent plus now the legal fees, depending on the State you're in, you can choose to accept it and stop the eviction process. You can bet they probably won't be late again once they realize you don't play around. Or, if they do it again, you can refuse to accept their late payment and just go ahead and get them out and get someone who isn't going to cause you headaches into the property. You could avoid all this by just letting the property manager stay in place. You aren't planning to make any extra monthly money with this property anyways. Don't take on the headaches and stress either. Remember, this is supposed to be the low stress way to retirement.

SET IT AND FORGET IT

Okay, you bought your property, you have a tenant in place, now it's time to put a reminder in your calendar for a year from now. For the next eleven months you just go on with life as normal, make a savings account and set money aside, as well as any left over rent money, if there is any, so you can build a down payment for the next house. In one year's time you are going to do this all over again. Diligently find a house that will make a good rental, buy it, put a tenant in it and hopefully forget about it unless you've elected to do the property management yourself. Remember to put savings aside again for the next down payment for the following year.

You continue doing this, adding one house to your portfolio a year for 15 years. When you are a real estate investor, it gets harder and harder to find loans for your next property because you are getting one loan after another week after week with no equity paydown seen and not much payment history under your belt before you are requesting yet another loan. With this process, your equity has time to build before you go requesting a loan for another house. Your credit score will increase or remain steady because of the mortgage payments, ensuring the loan process remains easy or becomes even easier. Your equity, which equates to your net worth, builds over the years also making it easier and easier to get a loan. Never go over the 30 day late mark, and there may be "No Doc" loans or "Stated Income" loans that your mortgage broker can help you get in future years.

If you can choose the time of year to buy, I would choose the August thru January time frame. People tend to look for new houses in the spring and like to be settled into their new house before school starts. This means there are a lot more people looking at and making offers on houses between mid-February through June or July. You want to buy when there are less people putting in offers so you can offer less than list price, if possible. Some locations of the country you may not be able to offer lower, but hopefully, if you buy during the quieter time in the market you won't have to be chasing the deal by offering above asking. The main thing is just to start. If it's February when you are reading this book, you may forget or lose the feeling that "Wow, this is an amazing plan!" and then forget to institute it when July rolls around. And remember, after talking to a mortgage broker, which is the first step, you may find that they want you to institute a program for 60 days that will move your credit score to a point where they can get you a better mortgage deal. If you wait before starting things could snowball and it could be another 4 months or so before you can get closed and all the sudden you are back into the springtime. Don't wait. Get started. And in the following years you can extend your "year" to 13 months for a couple of years until you are into July or August then hold steady at 12 months.

WHERE DID THE TIME GO

So fifteen years have passed and you now have 15 houses. Your next question is, "Okay, how do I retire?" My answer is, "Well remember that 15 year loan you took out on the first house that the tenants paid off for you over the past 15 years? It IS paid off! You now have a free and clear property."

"How does one free and clear property make me a six-figure income?" you ask? Yup, I get it. The rent would have to be over $8k a month just to get you to $100,000 in a year.

Well what if you refinanced the property? So now you can go and pull money back out of the property that you can again have the tenants pay off for you over the next 15 years. Depending on the value of the property, you could be a good deal higher than the amount rent would have given you each month. And guess what? You do not pay income taxes on money taken out from a loan. It is not classified as income, it is a loan.

For the sake of an example, say you bought a $200,000 home 15 years ago. Now let's say it's worth $225,000. That is conservative in this day and age after 15 years. If you refinance for 70% of value, that is $157,500. Can you live on $157,500 tax free money for a year? Even if you made $160,000 working your W2 job, after paying all your taxes you wouldn't have taken home $157,500 in a year. And if you only made the median United States household income of $74,202 as it is at the time of this writing, you would be effectively more than doubling your yearly living capital in retirement. And you'll still have 30% equity in the property.

As the cost of living goes up, property values go up. If the cost of living goes down, your property value may go down for that year. Either way, it will keep up with being able to sustain you each year, I would argue better than the stock market which can take years to come back after a bad bear market.

ANOTHER INFUSION OF TAX FREE MONEY

You will continue to do this each year. As the next property gets paid off, you take out another tax free money loan that your tenants will pay off for you. See why I said to try to keep it around the same month each year? With only a once a year income disbursement, you'll need to budget throughout the year so you don't run out before the year runs out. Many people will actually make more per year on this non-taxable money than they made working each year of the 15 year plan.

Make sure to put money into your properties, keeping them up to standards so you can have quality tenants. This will also help the value of your houses to increase with age instead of decrease because of maintenance issues. And unlike some retirement plans where you may run low on funds as you get closer to the end of life period, you may actually make more money each year as appreciation continues to grow. Take the example above, in another 15 years that house may now be worth $250,000 and 70% of that would be $175,000. Imagine getting more money each year the further into retirement you go. You will be able to keep up with inflation better than any other wealth building vehicle I can think of. So remember to talk with your property manager each year as you are going through the refinancing process. It will be a good idea to give them some of the money each year for a face lift or upgrade to your property between tenants. This house is taking care of you, make sure you take care of it.

And what a legacy you can pass down to your heirs teaching them this plan and leaving them the properties!

EXCELLENT OPTIONS

There are a few more suggestions I would like to make before we end here.

One, before you quit your W2 job, buy one more property, a 16th investment property. It will be harder to get a mortgage after you leave your W2 job, so do this right before you officially retire. I like this plan because, as the years progress, you'll eventually have one free and clear house that you won't need to refinance money out of for living expenses. The rent from this free and clear house will ensure your property manager stays in the positive with cash flow when major expenses happen as the houses get older. When you are sipping iced tea on a cruise in the Mediterranean, enjoying the sun, you don't want to hear from your property manager that a new furnace is required and your holding account is just shy of the total funds needed. This property will help you so you can keep more spending money for yourself each year.

Here is the second option. Maybe you just don't want to live so financially tight for 15 years making sure you are saving for down payments and property repairs that you elect to do 20 year mortgages rather than 15 year mortgages while you are working this program. This will lower your mortgage payments giving a bit more wriggle room in the rent. I still wouldn't take any excess funds, if there is any, as spending money. Remember, you must save for the next down payment. In today's market I've even heard of 18 year mortgages. Whatever works for you when you are running your numbers of rent against mortgage, taxes and insurance and maintenance against your income and what you are willing to do to get to retirement. Pick a time frame and work it. Make sure you add one house a year, around the same month mark as the year before.

SOME FINAL NOTES

I was a bookkeeper by trade before I became a real estate investor. It would not suit my nature not to circle back around to something I said in the beginning. If you cannot handle the idea of talking about taxes, then you can put the book down now and I will still feel good knowing you now have the concept of how to retire quicker than any other means I know of out there. But if you do take the time to read a few minutes more, then you will know a few more tips for saving money through the years. There is a reason that 90% of millionaires either made their money in real estate or hold their money in real estate, the tax savings and write offs allowed in real property.

If you use a property manager, they will give you a statement at the end of each year that you can use when doing your taxes. If you are managing your properties yourself, at least until you officially retire, make sure you keep very good records and receipts on expenses. I highly recommend using a CPA to do your taxes after you start buying real estate. Roofing, furnaces, flooring, everything can get depreciated at different time frames and only someone accustomed to doing taxes for real estate investors can get you the best deductions. Even the interest you pay on your mortgage, which is putting money back into your property so you can use it again, tax free, has a write off percentage. That is all I have to say on the matter. Use professionals, realtors, mortgage brokers, and tax professionals. It will save you from giving up on the plan before you hit retirement.

Remember insurance. If you have a loan against the property, you will have to maintain insurance. Don't let it lapse even if you keep a property free and clear and don't pull money back off of it. I know one investor who did and the tenant had a fire. They were managing their own property and didn't take the time to make sure their tenant had renters insurance in place. A property management company probably would have required this. Anyway, they were responsible for having to pay out of pocket to rebuild the home. And the city gave them a time frame for when it had to be done. It wasn't like they were able to say "Oh well, no rent here" and just leave it. I myself had two small fires in my properties. One that was in the kitchen of one property and one that was in the bedroom of another property from a tenant that was smoking in bed and fell asleep. Fires do happen. And that is what insurance is for. Make sure your property is always insured. You don't have to over insure it, do not insure it for the purchase price as that includes the ground the house is sitting on. The ground may become scorched, but it can never disappear. Grass can grow back. Just insure the house for what it would cost to build a house to replace it. Your insurance agent should be able to help you with that.

THE CONCLUSION

I hope you found this plan informative and doable. And a lot more secure than some other methods. I'm not against stock investing, or even other types of investments for that matter. But a house is steady and strong. It will never go out of business or have a CEO drive it into the ground.

I wish you joy and happiness as I know you will already have the abundance when you put this plan into action. Please leave me a review if you liked this book to encourage others to read it and take control of their retirement. Thank you.